DEAR STRANGER / THE WAYFARER

DEAR STRANGER / THE WAYFARER

Poems

by

Ralph C. Hamm III

Little Red Cell Publishing
New London, Connecticut. 06320

Copyright © 1979 & 2014 Ralph Conrad Hamm III

All rights for this book are reserved under International and Pan-American Copyright Conventions. Except for brief passages quoted in a newspaper, magazine, radio or television review, no part of this book may be reproduced in any form or by any means, electronic or mechanical, including photocopying and recording, or by any information storage and retrieval system, without permission in writing from the author and publisher.

First Edition, 2014, manufactured in USA
1 2 3 4 5 6 7 8 9 10 LSI 20 19 18 17 16 15 14

Set in Arial, Perpetua and Trajan Pro

Photograph of Ralph Conrad Hamm used by kind permission of the author.

Front cover painting called "Silence" (1911) by Odilon Redon (born Bertrand-Jean Redon; French: [April 20, 1840 – July 6, 1916).

Book Layout and Cover Design:
Michael J Linnard, MCSD

Library of Congress Cataloging-in-Publication Data:

Hamm, Ralph Conrad.
  Dear Stranger—The Wayfarer / by Ralph Conrad Hamm, III. -- 1st ed.
     p. cm.
  Includes Index.
  ISBN 978-1-935656-81-4 (pbk. : alk. paper)
  I. Poetry. II. Title.
  PS3623.O664S93 2014
  811'.6--dc22

Little Red Cell Publishing
New London, Connecticut, USA
www.littleredcell.com

Dedication

Life is essentially a viewpoint, through or by which, we helplessly observe everyone and everything that we love die.

And so, this specific assemblage of poetry will always be dedicated to the loving memory of my three year old nephew William David Van Ryzin — whose young life was sacrificed to cancer, due to the unfathomable religious tenets of my sister… his mother.

Acknowledgement

Gratitude to my mother, Margaret E. Hamm; my sisters, Marilyn Santiago and Glaydys Hamm; Ted Thomas, Jr., and, of course, Margaret Anne Strodder. Inspirations all — without whose love, assistance, and friendship, I would never have made it this far.

To the universal prisoner — the victim of avarice, racism, sexism, and genocide.

Contents

Introduction by Ted Thomas, Jr. and Margaret Anne Strodder	xiv
Dear Stranger / The Wayfarer	2
Preserves	4
I am Somebody	5
Phoenix	9
Thunder in the Transkei	11
The Ballad of Eritrea	13
The First Book of Mankind Called Oblivion	16
The Tinderbox	20
Pink or Blue	21
David's Song	23
Satan's Sunrise Serenade	24
Mass(achusetts) Sanitation	25
A Hymn...Sung Black for the Bicentennial.	26
A Bi-nonsense-terminal Message	31
Sphynx	33
A Constant Reminder Merits One Shining Example	34
D Implications of One	37
One of the Greatest Stories Never Told	38
The Coloring Book	41
Connect the Dots...Subject: Filling the Bill	42
Happy Horrorday	44
Kwanza...When I Could Not Be With Them	48
It's Roomy	50
Solitary	51
The Raven's Might	52
The Price of Recognition	55
From Where I Live	56
Corporate Directives	57
Teardroppings	58
In Memorial	59
Index of Titles and First Lines	61
About the Author	65

Author's Note

Somebody once said that the more things change the more they stay the same; thus, it is in the reading of *Dear Stranger/The Wayfarer*. Although written in the nineteen-seventies, when I was in my twenties and fighting for my very survival in the then touted most dangerous prison (per capita) in America—Walpole State Prison in South Walpole, Massachusetts—the reflections and socio-political/economic realities of that bygone era depicted within my poetry linger on today at the reprinting (new edition) of this collection in 2014.

No longer twenty years old, in many instances the circumstances expressed within the 1979 edition as foreboding have exacerbated, and are more vivid than ever today at the age of sixty-two.

In some of my earliest poems I replaced the capital "I" with the lower case "i," in what I deemed a creative effort to render my ego insignificant.

The obvious change to the original manuscript of 1979 is the addition of drawings and sketches, which I have included to afford a visual representation of my political/social reality yesterday and today.

Peace & Blessings

Aluta continuaa!

INTRODUCTION

[reprinted from the 1979 edition]

It may be that for many people who have not yet met him, Ralph Hamm is a figment of their imagination. He acknowledges that possibility in the first poem of this his first collection of poems. Yet, for those of us who have met and come to know this extraordinary young man, the authenticity of his existence can never be dented — nor can the conditions of prison, a major theme in this book.

It is not just that he writes about prison—where he has spent last ten years of his life—but that he does it well. His style is sometimes forceful and impolite, crashing its way into our collective consciousness; but we will be all the better for that. More often his style is descriptive. He tells us that a sunrise in prison is a condition where:

> *"Remnants of a dream*
> *or the eve's nightmare,*
> *linger in stale, grey cigarette smoke*
> *and rank, starchy pubic hair..."*

It is exactly so that prisons are stale, grey places; we know that much. What Mr. Hamm does in his metaphor is to remind us that the physical conditions of prisons often produce a corresponding spiritual condition in the "inmates" held in them. This then is the responsibility of the prison poet, and poets in general, to resist such a "descent into hell" and to urge his comrades to do the same. Poets in prison, we think, may know that more than other poets. There are times when the poet in prison, because he is where he is, feels alone and forgotten. Indeed, the imprisoned poet may have to ask his fellows, from whom he has been removed:

> "Remember me?
> The boy who tried to reach
> but my hand was slapped
> tried to strike back
> but my arm was trapped."

And finally, because we on the outside have been quiet for so long, and perhaps for no other confirmation but his own, the poet cries out, "I am alive." From time to time such exclamations are necessary, not only because it may help the imprisoned maintain their sanity, but because they may help the rest of us to regain ours.

There are times, revealed here in this book, when a kind of loneliness we may never know grips Mr. Hamm. Yet he does not beg our sympathy, he doesn't really want us to feel sorry for him; what he wants us to do is hear him. He wants us to allow ourselves to become his Dear Stranger.

Oh, there is anger here and there is this book. But we can allow for that, can't we, given the circumstances of Mr. Hamm's life? He was, after all, locked in solitary confinement when he became 21 — that important transitional period in a young man's life, usually accompanied by celebration. But for Ralph Hamm there was no particular celebration, except:

> "….the cries of misery…
> the cries of frustrated anger…
> and the ever present sound

of countless cell doors
clanging
echoing."

Perhaps the most admirable quality of Mr. Hamm's work is that it finally transcends the immediate experience of prison life. It is difficult to transcend his immediate circumstances. We can only imagine what energy must be put into the effort it takes for an imprisoned poet to move, as it were, outside of the walls. Mr Hamm does that and many of his poems reflect his concern and awareness of world conditions that directly affect black people and indirectly everyone.

Read this book. It is about a man who has come to terms with himself in a hostile environment. It is about coming of age and growth and development. It is about hope and love and strength. It is about a man his life and his vision. Do it. Read this book. Begin by saying, Ralph Hamm, III wants to talk with me, then allow yourself to hear him say, "Dear Stranger..."

Ted Thomas, Jr.
Margaret Anne Strodder
Boston, May, 1979

DEAR STRANGER / THE WAYFARER

Dear Stranger/The Wayfarer

I am
a figment of your imagination-
love's ever-allusive ideal;
but for that particular/peculiar reason
you are unable to see me,
and you cannot actually touch me.

You may never chance to know me
because of your fear,
and your denial,
of me; yet I
have weathered the storms
of time
to introduce myself to you.

I am what some say, "Has come!"
while others pray, "Has not come!"

I was in your mother's womb
beside you, then
took to the wind
to challenge the ages
along side of you.

I am
a father's pyre!

I am a son's desire!

I am
the means that are necessary!

I am
dreams lain broken and arbitrary!

I am
something old…
something new…
something refused,
            yet
something due.

Who am I!

I am
Life's Innuendo,
cast within a teardrop,
in umbra hue.

Preserves

The stains on your hands (all up under your nails)
are not there by chance,
but were sustained quite deliberately.
For in your quest to seize the nectar,
some tried to escape
in a frantic and desperate attempt to be free.

Once clinging to the ancestral bush,
from which others before had been plucked,
and fast gaining the status of delicacy;
our young unripened fruit
are canned to preserve their texture and flavor,
to sate the hunger and thirst of a cannibalistic society.

As your unrelinquishing grip
squeezes me tighter, I plead for release.
But what is the use?
My liquid soul and pulpy body have been rendered apart.
Now I seep through your fingers and run down your arm,
like wild blackberry juice.

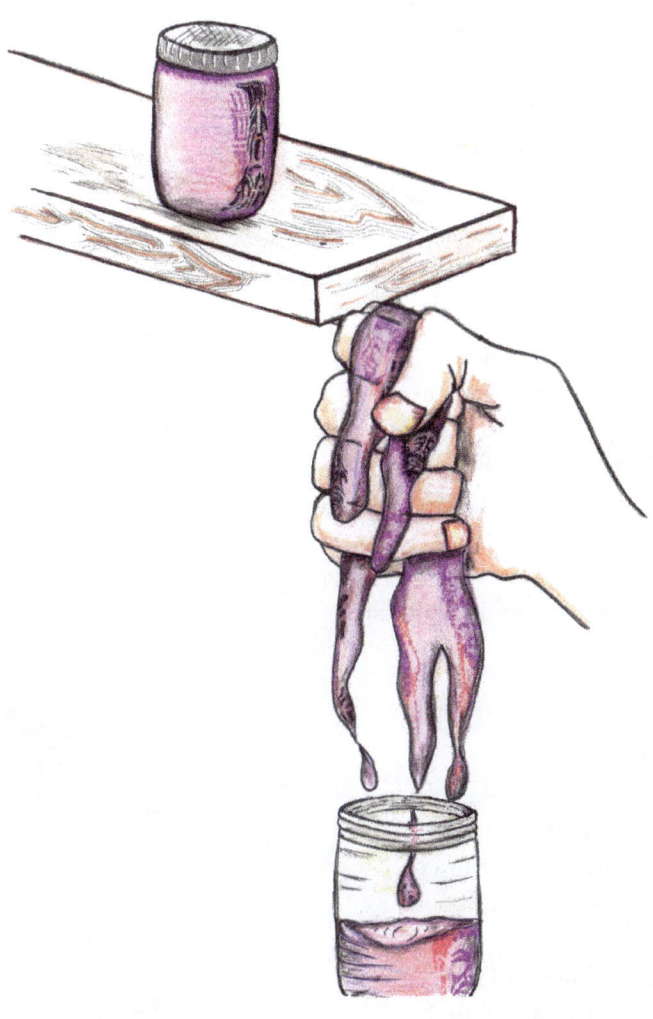

I am Somebody!

All through my childhood
I flew like the sparrow,
until the day I noticed
that I had no shadow,
I looked around myself
at my five sisters
and saw that they didn't
have shadows either.
In bewilderment I glanced
across the ghetto street,
and found nothing cast, except trash,
under Black children's feet.
I rushed home in panic
to evaluate the prospect
of the sun not reflecting
off a sold object.
I asked myself: "An I dreaming?"
Am I awake?
What is the answer,
for sanity's sake?"
So, on that day,
I decided my direction.
I would find the answer
to the burning question:
"Am I somebody?"

I told my friends of my decision,
and they said I was a fool.
And that I'd meet my death
if I broke the rules.
For nobody had crossed the boundary
between TRUTH and LIE,
to where one's dreams and ambitions
could reach the sky.
Few had ever succeeded

in locating their shadow,
and the few never returned to help the many
cross the LIE's straight and narrow.
But my destiny had been revealed
and I could not hide,
so I gathered up all of my strength
and crossed the GREAT DIVIDE.

LIFE changed its structure
from wrong to right,
as millions of shadows
were now in my sight.
I waved to the nearest person
and walked up to his face,
but his eyes reflected non-recognition
as they peered through my space.
I yelled my name!
I asked: "Can't you hear me?
Smell me? Feel me?
Fool! Can't you see me?"
I ran past him in horror,
and raced through a door
and found that I had run
into a suburban shopping mall store.
I went to the back
and located a mirror,
Then found out that my image
did not appear there!
I picked up a nearby chair...
made a pass...
and then I angrily threw it
through the looking-glass.
To my great surprise
three men stepped through.
They all worn badges
and were dressed in blue.
They slapped me in chains

and before I could yell,
I was convicted and imprisoned
in yet another Hell.
I believe it was at that moment
that I began to see
I had to do wrong in right
for them to notice me.

Now I am older
and I have been away for years,
but I have survived the crossing in Spirit—
so put aside your fears.
With time and wisdom
I have come to understand
that crime is not the only answer,
there is an even better one at hand.
So, here is the formula
to help pull you through…
it's a foolproof formula
that will add substance to you:
a) Know that you can become
    whatever you want to be,
    because your range is unlimited
    and your Spirit is free!
b) Place your mind
    into the proper perspective
    by setting a goal
    and then reaching its objective!
c) Raise your head
    above the clouds.
    Take a real deep breath,
    and then scream out loud:
    "WORLD, MAKE ROOM FOR ME—
    I AM SOMEBODY!
    DON'T LOOK THROUGH ME—
    I AM SOMEBODY!"

Phoenix

We played it well
But tripped and fell
Screaming and wailing in the agony of our descent
                                                  down
                                                  down
                                                  down

After what seemed an eternity
We reached bottom.
People walked by
And in desperation we called for help.
Yet no one heard
(or chose not to hear).
Having lost contact with those above
And the world.
The sands of time slowly sifted
And nobody passes now.
And the cold…
The hunger…
The darkness…
Have all become a part of our everyday existence.
But down
    down (there)
  …down (here)
We multiplied
With the hopes that in the near future
We will be able to create a ladder
Built from the bones
Of our predecessors
And the strength
Of our young…
To climb up
And rise up and out of our pitfall
Into a "new world"

As a new people.
Needing no aid…
Refusing all assistance
From those who posed
                paused
And vaunted themselves above us.

Thunder in the Transkei

Hear a rumbling to the south,
the sound of mountains falling?
Hear the bellow of cannon fire,
and a bugle's mournful calling?

Aboriginal young ladies of the evening
turn down Johns, Harrys, and Dicks,
while doggie treats are given to the World Press
for their will performed **politricks.**

Circling vultures cry overhead
and they flinch with pain,
as blood drops from mutant clouds
in the form of burning rain.

> There is Thunder in the Transkei;
> Watch the little children run
> for shelter from the storming
> of a lethal, smoking gun.

apartheid streets are all deserted,
foot prints cast by the die.
I look Eastward for my Brothers,
but I get "Blood in My Eye."

Mannequins guard boarded storefronts,
bayonets fixed and standing at parade rest.
They're all sworn to protect inhumanity's false securities
with their final plastic breath.

Lightning flashes brilliant yellow,
making silicone skin perspire,
and surrounding shrouded suburban townships

within a solid ring of all-consuming fire.

        There is Thunder in the Transkei;
        watch the little children run
        for shelter from the storming
        of a lethal, smoking gun.

gutters overflow with, and from, accumulation,
telephone poles fall and communications fail.
For the drops of blood have solidified
and now descend as grey lead hale.

The oppressor panics within the **darkness**,
terrified by sights never before espied.
Christian church bells toll the numbers dead
from South Afrikaan industrial strength suicide.

Gale winds increase in intensity
as sounds, sights, and actions unite,
and Ian Smith fiddles while Pretoria burns-
marking the the beginning of End's night!

        There is Thunder in the Transkei;
        watch the little children run
        for shelter from the storming
        of a lethal, smoking gun.

2-7-78 11:30 p.m.

Reclining in my cage...listening to the news on the radio. Ethiopian and Cuban forces, with the aid of Russian MIG jet fighters and naval vessels, have laid siege upon the Eritrean revolutionary forces in Eritrea. (A war that the American news media stresses is being fought solely against Somalia.) The history of the armed struggle can be summed up thusly: All of the world powers want control of the Afars seaport to monitor the traffic of the Suez Canal. The Eritrean people are the only obstacle standing in the way of that control, and they presently find themselves in an armed struggle to keep from being liquidated. Truth always seems to thrust up into the face of history the sordid fact that Africans will kill Africans for the sake (monetary benefit) of Imperialism. Africa's historical pain, sorrow, and indignation will hopefully be expressed within the lines of this poem...

The Ballad of Eritrea

Ancestral spirits spiral up from smoking hamlets —
Somalia bears witness to the dread.
Freedom haunts the bomb-charred landscape,
mourning children of the dead.

Terror flies, full mast, at days end!
Metallic birds-of-prey fill the air.
Human predators seek their nightly carrion,
and combat each other for a share.

Africa weeps her bitter moisture,
like so many times before...
moltern tears flow into the Red Sea,
from Afars' sun-baked and embattled shore.

>O Eritrea! Eritrea!
>Suez lies vitally upon the sea-
>Africans lie mortally upon the sand.

>O Eritrea! Eritrea!
>Your offspring are bellowing in torment-
>soothe those brethren if you can.

Blue water flows to nourish the seed,
and to ensure a fertile life.
Blue waters carried the "hammer and sickle"
that butchered humanity with its knife.

SEE: The little girl who lost Tomorrow
staring vacantly up into space.
The blasphemous shadow of a Russian MIG
has marred forever the beauty of her face.

Screaming thunder from the heavens!
The bowels of nature are burst asunder.
Imperialist nations sing: Glory hallelujah!
rejoicing in the pirate's plunder.

> O Eritrea! Eritrea!
> Suez lies vitally upon the sea-
> Africans lie mortally upon the sand.

> O Eritrea! Eritrea!
> Your offspring are bellowing in torment-
> soothe those brethren if you can.

Desert skeletons remain poised in battle
with the sun, that's bleaching metal and bone.
Propaganda rests, perched upon Lie's dung heap,
and Truth mans Fate's sentry-post alone.
Foreign soldiers attack the left flank-
foreign mercenaries advance on the right.
Death nestles in the warmth of a mother's bosom,
suckling on the withered nipples of her fright.

Raise the torch that proclaims your liberation!
Hold your banners of fortitude high!
DAWN: The sandy tract now crimson-
tinted by the Red Sea tide.

O Eritrea! Eritrea!
Suez lies vitally upon the sea-
Africans lie mortally upon the sand.

O Eritrea! Eritrea!
Your offspring are bellowing in torment-
soothe those brethren if you can.

The First Book of Mankind Called Oblivion

In the beginning
man discovered iron and mined for ore.
2 And the ore was smelted and the gun was formed.
And the design of the gun moved
across the face of the earth.
3 And mankind said: "Let there be war!"
and there was war.
4 And mankind saw the war, and that it was profitable,
and mankind defined gaining and losing profit.
5 And mankind called the gaining GOOD,
and the losing he called BAD.
And the scheming and the deceiving
were the first stage.
6 And mankind said: "Let there be the lie
in the midst of the truth,
and let it hide the truth from the people!"
7 And mankind made the lie and hid the truth,
which could have liberated the people,
and it was so.
8 And mankind called the lie DEMOCRACY (demon-rule).
And the scheming and the deceiving
were the second stage.
9 And mankind said: "Let the young men at eighteen
be gathered together unto one place,
and let the barracks appear!" and it was so.
10 And mankind called the barracks FORT;
And the gathering together of the young men
he called ARMY,
and mankind saw that it was GOOD.
11 And mankind said: "Let the ARMY bring forth gain,
the aboriginal people yielding slave labor
and their lands yielding natural resources,
who wealth is in itself upon the face of the earth!"

and it was so.
12 And the ARMY brought forth gain,
the aboriginal peoples yielding slave labor
and their lands yielding natural resources,
whose wealth is in itself;
and mankind saw that it was GOOD.
13 And the scheming and the deceiving
were the third stage.
14 And mankind said: "Let there be world powers,
in apparent opposition to the world,
to divide the earth into western and eastern hemispheres,
and let them be for signs and for seasons,
and for days and years;
15 And let them be for rulership of the heavens
to help subjugate the peoples of the earth!
and it was so.
16 And mankind made two great world powers;
the greater power to rule the west,
and the apparently lesser power to rule the east;
they made colonies and satellite states also.
17 And mankind set their eyes
to the firmament of the heavens
to gain supremacy of the skies;
18 And to rule over the west and over the east
and to terrorize and hide the truth from the people,
and mankind saw that it was GOOD.
19 And the scheming and the deceiving
were the fourth stage.
20 And mankind said: "Let the waters bring forth abundantly
the underwater ships and surface carriers
and the airplanes that may fly above the earth
in the open firmament of heaven!"
21 And mankind created great under water submarines
and water surface naval carriers and every kind of vessel
that moves, which the waters brought forth abundantly

after their kind
and every sort of airplane after its kind;
and mankind saw that it was GOOD.
22 And mankind blessed their NAVY and AIR FORCE, saying:
"Be fruitful, and multiply, and fill the waters
in the seas, and let the armed forces multiply on the earth!"
23 And the scheming and the deceiving
were the fifth stage.
24 And mankind said: "Let the airplane
and the submarine bring forth the atomic bomb,
the hydrogen bomb and the nuclear missile after its kind!"
and it was so.
25 And mankind made the atomic bomb,
the hydrogen bomb and the nuclear missile after its kind;
and mankind saw that it was GOOD.
26 And mankind said: "Let us teach our children
in our image, after our lifestyle
and let them have dominion over the ships of the sea
and over the planes and missiles of the air
and over the aboriginal people
and over all of the earths' resources
and over every creeping thing that creeps
upon the earth!"
27 So mankind taught their children in their own image,
in the image of themselves taught they them
male and female alike taught they them.
28 Hence, mankind had cursed them,
when mankind said unto them: "Be fruitful,
and multiply profit
and ravish the earth and subdue it;
and have domination through the ships of the sea
and through the planes and missiles of the air
and rule with an iron fist
over every living thing that moves upon the earth!"
29 And mankind saw everything that they had made

and, behold, it was VERY GOOD.
And the scheming and the deceiving
were the sixth stage.
30 Thus freedom within the heavens and the earth was finished.
31 After the subjugation of the world population
and the depletion of the earths' natural resources
and the pollution of the environment,
mankind passed on the inheritance.
And the children had been programmed
to believe that it all was GOOD.
32 And during the seventh stage,
due to callousness, wanton destruction, greed
and mankind's inhumanity to man,
mankind ended…
themselves.

Tinderbox

From childhood, society drills into man's head
that he must struggle alone for life's daily bread.
And woman's position is thus clearly defined
to be one step ahead of man, yet four steps behind!

There isn't enough room for husband and wife to grow
and within this vacuum they must reap what they sow.
So, in mortal combat these two lost souls abide
separated by egoism, fear and foolish pride.

Their children would watch in horror and despair,
as strife and physical violence pulled apart their parental pair.
The parents couldn't see in their children's tears
how their separation would affect the children in later years.

So, you want to build a home!
Is your foundation sunk on stone?
Because if life doesn't settle like it should,
time will find a tinderbox where a family once stood…
              gone, gone house of wood.

Pink or Blue

got letter tonight
in a pink envelope with my mother's name on it.
my heart was filled
with the joy of expectation.

got a letter tonight
and removed the pink leaves of paper
from their pink confinement.
the sun
filtered through the open window
and the pages of my letter
reflected the bars
of my prison cell.
it was my sister...
the letter read:
      "Howdy Lil' Bro.
      Comin' to you from Mass. General Clinic
      is the uncomparable me."... S
                                  H
                                  A
                                  D
                                  O
                                  W

      "Well for family news Aunt Pearlee called
      and your Aunt Miggie.
      Jamie was found dead
      in Cambridge 6 mos. ago."...S
                                  H
                                  A
                                  D
                                  O
                                  W
      "Ruthie was in Germany in the hospital

but at the time no one could find her.
Your father was found dead
in Trinidad Colorado."... S
                        H
                        A
                        D
                        O
                        W

"After we leave here
mom and I are going to S.S. and the Veteran's Admin.
it will cost around 500 dollars.
Ma wants to know
if you want to attend the services
at the Mattapan V.A. center." ... S
                                       H
                                       A
                                       D
                                     O
                                     W

got a letter tonight
in a pink envelope with my mother's name on it.
my heart
    was filled
        with the joy of expectation.

David's Song

Cry if he's gone,
but don't allow bad
feelings to keep you down.
Fonder moments cling
to eternal memory vines-thorny,
yet soft as feather down.

Cry! And allow those tears
to flow, watering
life's fertile ground.
It is but early Spring-
the time for sowing
where dreams abound.

Sigh, in knowing that
if he leaves us
he'll still carry on-again.
For nothing dies...
not even the tumultuous
winds of a hurricane.

Sighing eternal love,
his voice will echo
like the Lorelei's melodic refrain-
As the endless sands
of our time shift to reunite
us all on another plane.

Satan's Sunrise Serenade
(or Morning's Promise)

As the sun
surmounts the eastern wall
and the crows
signal the breakfast call,
eyelids will crack
the caked-on night
and the crust will decay into powder
in the morning light.

Remnants of a dream
or the eve's nightmare,
linger in stale grey cigarette smoke
and rank, starchy pubic hair.
They are the secret affairs
of sterile-life men,
who may never live
to love again.

Cold water is splashed
to awaken deadened skin
and to refresh the soul
that lies sealed within.
A baleful scream
is made to appear as jest,
yet purposed to give sanity
its endurance test.

Static energy charges
from cell to cell,
as the body, damned, begins
another day in Hell.

Mass(achusetts) Sanitation

I cried from the gutter
allowing the tears
to wash to sewage from my face.
with strained, stiff-jointed effort
I raised my head
to separate myself from the old news-
                      papers
                      spittle
                      assorted garbage
                      and discarded cigarette butts…
…reached for the pedestrian curb
for assistance in my upliftment.
accidently (?)
my hand was stepped upon
and I was noticed-
though recognized
not to be of any value…
regarded as trash
and thrown into a refuse bin

        labelled: "KEEP AMERIK.K.K.A. CLEAN."

A Hymn...Sung Black for the Bicentennial

Oh listen youth
hark unto me—
to the tune
that I will sing…
        A shocking refrain
        to make you see
        through years
        and tears that sting.

A message crooned
that must be heard—
a tale
that must be sung…
        Bruised lips
        that utter alien words
        like burrs
        which tear the tongue.

My song is like a funeral dirge,
the tune is not sweet nor mellow.
I sing my song to **future** ears,
because the **present** is **past** my bellow.

First
    herded upon Hawkins' "Jesus" ship
To die
    in the cargo hold.
Ravaged
    torn and bled under slavery's whip—
Displayed
    then sold BLACK GOLD.
Brought
    to the land of democracy

In violation
    of Africa's womb.
Lynched
    upon the revered "liberty tree"—
Settled dust
    in the Ameriklan tomb.

(Fredrick Douglass said that the old slaves sang chorus:
              "We raise de wheat
      dey gib us corn
            we bake de bread
      dey gib us crust
            we sif de meal
      de gib us huss
            we peal de meat
      dey gib us skin
            and dat's de way
      dey take us in.
            We skim de pot
      dey gib us liquor
            and say dat's good eh nuff
      for de nigguh.")

Stripped
    of all of our heritage and pride—
Made
    to wallow in "master's" vomit.
Felt
    the cold steel blade of genocide
and the racial hate
    that soon followed it.
Went off
    to fight for him in two world wars—
Not to forget
    revolutionary…civil…and "Nam."

Returned
    still the victim of racial bars—
Ameriklan justice
    and her mighty arm.

(Fredrick Douglass said that the old slaves sang chorus:
        "We raise de wheat
    dey gib us corn
        we bake de bread
    dey gib us crust
        we sif de meal
    de gib us huss
        we peal de meat
    dey gib us skin
        and dat's de way
    dey take us in.
        We skim de pot
    dey gib us liquor
        and say dat's good ch nuff
    for de nigguh.")

Now
    ghettoized and stigmatized—
Just up
    from chattel slavery.
How long
    will I stand to be victimized
Before
    I gain the self urge to be free?
Brands
    to make me animal class—
Mental
    chains about my head.
200 years
    a tortured mass—

Robbed,
    maimed and left for dead.

My song was like a funeral dirge,
the tune not sweet nor mellow.
I sang my song to future ears,
because the present was past my bellow.

The Stranger / The Wayfarer

A Bi-Nonsense-Terminal Message

(Fredrick Douglass' message/speech given at Rochester, New York on July 3, 1852. Put into rhyme by this poet for July 4, 1976. In the transition of the speech, words have been added and deleted for the context to fit present day circumstances and for the rhyme to make sense.)

Amerik.k.k.a the free?
Please excuse me,
but what you are implying doesn't make much sense.
What have I to do
or those that I represent, too,
with the exaltation of your national independence?

Are the principles that you run
of political freedom
and of natural justice extended to us,
or are we called upon to bring
our humble offerings and sing
in the back of a stone ruptured
and blood spattered school bus?

What to the Ameriklan slave
is your Fourth of July charade,
but just another day to suffer through?
Shuffling to the song
that has had us muted for so long—
"America!" the red, white, and blue.

Your celebration is a sham,
but you don't give a damn
because your breast is full of national pride and vanity.
Through the wars that you have fought,
the lies, brutality and hatred you have taught
that national pride reeks of cultural insanity.

The semantics are strange
from your mind/mouth disarranged—
raising shouts of justice, liberty and equality.
With prayers and hymns,
sermons and unholy Thanksgivings…
not to forget the parade and solemnity.

Through the facade I see
your celebration to be
more bombast, a fraud, cloak and dagger deception.
Yet in everyone's face
you tend to flaunt your disgrace
as man's much sought after, and now acquired, perfection.

There is not a nation on earth
that recognizes your birth
as anything other than modern day Babylon.
For behind false avowals
and underneath klansmen cowls
lies the identity of a whoremongering throng.

Travel where you may…
roam and search everyday
through the civilizations of the old and new world.
Look for all that is evil
but you'll find none the rival
of you and that star spangled funeral shroud that you've unfurled.

To profess the benefits bestowed
and to express our gratitude
for two-hundred years of oppression since independence?!!
Well Amerik.k.k.a at best
I truly must confess that it still doesn't make much sense.

Sphynx

Inspired wisdom of the sages.
Epical breath of yore.
Impregnable rock of the ages.
Stone Lion! Roar!

A Constant Reminder Merits One Shining Example

1.
A baby's cry
pierces through the wintry night.
Is he crying from hunger,
from cold or sudden fright?
This new born babe
escaping his mother's womb...
a crying ghetto baby
in a laughing ghetto tomb!

    The child is growing
    he is now a little boy
    in a steel and concrete reality
    the likes of which destroys
    his creativity,
    his love...his will to "be."
    He looks familiar—
    doesn't he resemble you and me?

You'll see him run run run!
I'll see him run run run!
What will make him run run run?
Well, he'll be running through Hell.

2.
During six years of schooling
he is taught things not of his own.
Portrayed as a slave and outcast
he rejects it then runs away from home.
But man is a communal animal
and naturally clannish prone...
the street gang becomes his "adopted" family—
he'd die if out alone.

> Them asphalt streets are hungry
> they consume unwary prey.
> So he begins to roam at night
> and shuns the light of day.
> That's him there fighting;
> his wits keep him alive…
> there is no mistaking
> his motive to survive.

You see him run run run!
I see him run run run!
What makes him run run run?
Well, he's running through Hell.

3.
Now battle fatigued and weary—-
unable to please the "war" god.
He replaces his knife for a needle
and falls off in to a nod.
Do you hear that high pitched screaming?
It seems to be getting louder.
Is it from the pain or pleasure
brought on by snow white powder?

> His senses have become diverted
> by the monkeys he has to feed.
> He can't see the rats nor roaches,
> now blinded to society's greed.
> Won't someone please help him—
> reach out a steady hand—
> or is he to become a new statistic
> in Amerik.k.k.a's "family welfare plan?"

You see him run run run!
I see him run run run!

      What makes him run run run?
      He's running through Hell.

4.
A shrill siren
shrieks through the ghetto night.
Was someone beat or robbed;
is there a fire nearby to fight?
There is no telling
so many are heard each day.
Yet within every ear-splitting wail
you can hear his momma pray.

      As night continues to descend
      he is nowhere to be found.
      Hey, but what is that in the alley
      in a heap upon the ground?
      That is our brother in there dead—
      lying flat upon his face!
      Just as he passes/a cry/a birth
      and another synonymous life takes his place.

You see him run run run!
I see him run run run!
What makes him run run run?
Well, he's running through Hell!!

D Implications of One

One is a solitary bird—
beaked pointed toward D sky.
One
seldom suffers for company.
Here are D reasons why:

        One
        can light D spark
        that ignites a prairie fire.
        One
        can stand D watch
        long after many, wearily, retire.

        One
        can find D path
        when others give up hope.
        One can lead D way
        with insight obtained through growth.

        One
        can subdue D heart
        and guarantee D soul's surrender.
        One
        can generate D force
        uniting the male/female genders.

        One
        was all by oneself
        before D universe had begun.

D One D-termined
can change D world,
for D with One
is DONE!

One of the Greatest Stories Never Told

Once upon a time there was a farmer,
whose ideal it was to feed the world community.
His heart furnished the seeds and cultivators
to produce enough food for eternity.

When a leadership position was placed upon his shoulders,
he implored various civic representatives for their help.
For within the fields the pests were getting bolder,
he knew that he couldn't cover all the acreage by himself.

He could recall his now deceased father saying:
"Son, it's now up to you get the job done.
Irregardless of how many of the people are playing,
instead of working toward our goal's completion."

So the brother asked them:
    "Why don't you hitch your horses to the wagon?
    Our seeds won't grow if we are lagging.
    Come on and let us pull together!
    It is easy if we pull together!
    We will each bear a portion of the sorrow,
    if we put it off and wait until tomorrow.
    You know we've got to pull together!
    We will make it if we pull together!"

A lot of his neighbors scorned what he was doing,
Saying: "What a fool he is to work the fields alone—"
Then a few friends rolled up their sleeves to help him,
the others watched them work their fingers to the bone.

Life for the idle was nothing but a party,
dancing, singing and lounging throughout the day.
Yet, the workers each seemed to possess the strength of forty!

As they nurtured the dreams that their convictions would pay.
Through drought, and torrential rain, they tilled the soil.
Farming from the dawn until the wee hours of the night
to produce the end product of all their toil—
knowing the suffering it would take to make things right.

So they sang:
    "We hitched our horses up to the wagon,
      to show the world that we weren't simply bragging.
    It's hard work, but we pull together!
    In harmony we pull together!
    No one has ever accomplished a thing by weeping,
    And dreams are not only for those who are sleeping.
    Wide awake we pull together!
    Our foresight helps us to pull together!"

As the days went by and winter crept upon them,
they worked even faster to get the crop in.
Their numbers had swelled in fulfilling the obligation.
They were pushing harder as time kept growing slim.

The jeers remained…the parties..and the laughter,
but not as much as the summer months before.
The hecklers could now see the goal that the farmers were after,
And the scene didn't seem that funny anymore.

Idlers are dying in drifts, left by winter snowstorms!
Scavengers are starving in snow covered and barren fields!
Very few can laugh, when hunger pangs are borne,
but others can sleep satisfied from nature's generous yield.

My moral is:
    "Hitch your horses up to the wagon.
    Life's harvest can't be reaped by lagging.
    People have to pull together!

As ONE they have to pull together!
We have to raise up ourselves from the social gutter,
by lending a steady hand unto our sister/brother.
We can make it, if we pull together!
RECREATE THE WORLD!
                Just pull together."

Coloring Book...Subject: Liberated Ghetto Child

Born and bred on a ghetto street—
struggling hard everyday just to survive.
Fighting rats and roaches for enough to eat
and hopefully to stay alive.

1. The system that refuses to give him slack.
2. The work that broke his father's back.
3. The small arms that display a junky's tracks.

                COLOR THEM BLACK!

Not being taught what is truly real,
he soon drops out of school.
Life to him is a game of beat, rob and steal;
or perish under the oppressor's rule.

4. The prostitutes, dope and mafia infested scene.
5. The pimps and pushers looking clean.
6. The long dope habit and lack of money have made him mean.

                COLOR THAT GREEN!

Now fully deprived of his will,
the white powder becomes his only steady diet.
In order to live, he now must kill—
to keep his monkeys quiet.

7. The tears that his mother and sisters shed.
8. The police that shot him in the head.
9. The bullet wounds from which he bled.

                COLOR THEM RED...
                        COLOR HIM DEAD!

Connect-the-Dots…Subject: Filling the Bill

We are living in the milk and honey land of democracy,
where people are "bred" by class, color, and race.
Justice is the blindfolded madame of hypocrisy,
her scale is a tool to keep all of the "niggers" in place.

1. The prisons are full of poor men and women serving time.
2. Black people are "class accused" for the rise in crime.
3. Unemployment means no jobs, although the workers are willing.

CONNECT THE DOLLAR SIGNS AND THEN FILL IN THE VILLAIN!

There isn't any money to make the **basic** ends meet,
due to the manipulated rise in the economy.
The poor prey upon each other, for sustenance, in city streets—
they are all victims of the super rich and multi–national industry.

4. 40,000 die annually from asbestos poisoning and in industrial accidents.
5. Greedy, murderous, slumlords collect insurance by torching tenements.
6. "Social Security" means dogfood to eat for the elderly men and women.

CONNECT THE DOLLAR SIGNS AND THEN FILL IN THE VILLAIN!

Our children are our future and a reflection of us—
they are also the inheritors of parent America's ill's.
With WASHINGTON, "E PLURIBUS UNUM," and
"IN GOD WE TRUST,"
there just isn't enough room for them beside the dollar bill.

7. Schools have become asylums designed by the truly criminally insane.
8. Humanity is drugged with "valium," to disguise the pain.
9. The flesh may survive, for it's the mind that they're killing.

CONNECT THE DOLLAR SIGNS AND THEN FILL IN THE VILLAIN!

Happy Horrorday
(or dashing to the bank, laughing all the way)

                1.

Santa Claus is coming to town!
With octopus tentacles
 that reach out,
(and leech onto their unsuspecting victims)
sufficiently sucking the life's blood
out of the poor.
Dig
some fat and bearded m.f.
telling you to buy a SUNBEAM this
and a WESTINGHOUSE that…
while you are fervently praying
for at least one sunbeam
(beamed down from the sun),
to warm the apartment
that you are residing in
on the west side of the housing projects.

2.
Away in a manger!
Damned if all of our children
aren't born in a stable…away in a manger.
In a dark
musty and damp corner of society
that is positively unfit
for human habitation,
(said the shepherd boy to the little lamb:
"tain't nuttin' hap'nin!"
A.S.P.C.A. would have him arrested
if he put his lamb through
what I go through)
There isn't enough money

in the state for welfare
(food stamps, day care, medicaid),
but there seems to be
ample enough money in the WELFARE STATE
to hire more police
to assist
in escorting and protecting
the rich, semi-rich and pseudo-rich…
as they move through the city's
under-priviledged areas…
("down town" Xmas shopping)
a testimony to the state
of their
and our welfare.

3.

Joy to the world!
Now tell me truthfully
(I know that everyone is caught up in the "spirit"),
what the hell have I got
to be joyful about?
Skyrocketing economy and unemployment?
My children
(all Black children are my children),
being stoned
either on the mind altering drugs
of television and heroin…
or on school buses?
Or children beaten in the school itself
and on the streets by bigoted police?
Maybe the ideology
that the children are raised up on…
believing in the tooth fairy,
the Easter bunny, and santa claus?
With the parents

unable to make good
on the payment of **presents**
through past delusions.

4.

It came upon a midnight clear!
No it wasn't a sleigh
(maybe eight "reigning dears")
with a little old driver
so fast and so quick
that I knew in a moment
that it must be Saint Nick.
Unless
Saint Nick happens to be the dude
that owns the shipping lines,
whose freighter just docked-in this morning
and unloaded three million dollars
worth of uncut heroin.
What did come
came in clear glassine bags
which were delivered upon midnight
(eastern standard time)
to thousands
of school children
throughout the inner city,
(and he shall reign for ever and ever
Hallelujah! Hallelujah! Hal le lu jah!!)

5.

Oh Christmas tree—oh Christmas tree!
Of course I am referring to
the tree outside of the White House.
(you know—the one in D.C.)
The one that costs
two-hundred and fifty-thousand dollars

just to keep it lit…
and I helped pay for it
with my tax dollars,
(I'm broke now…no rebate)
I can now see
that Santa Claus
is only jolly ole Uncle Sam
in a "not-so-really-different"
suit of clothes.
Notice
how in both instances
we eventually end up paying
for all of those **treats**
that he doles out
of his bag…of **tricks**?
Tricks or treats?
TREATS FOR TRICKS!?
Naw.
That's an entirely different holiday altogether…
isn't it?

Kwanza...When I Could Not Be With Them

As they sang,
"LIFT EVERY VOICE AND SING..."
I was not with them...
but was out of bounds
peeking
through an adjourning door into time.
When the cry,
"UMOJA"
was raised in a clenched fist salute,
I was not with them...
but was standing
with my palms open by my side
where years of betrayal and mistrust
had them manacled together.

Then the seven candles were lit.
And as each match kissed its designated wick
the darkness of the room
was gradually bathed
in light,
I saw the mark of the "beast"
on Black foreheads...
and fear
in once proud eyes,
while in the background
two prison guards grinned
as the brothers and sisters
continued
with their game of charades.

I transcended the celestial plain then
and became a recited verse...
synonymous with the eulogies

of Turner, Garvey, Lumumba,
Malcolm X, Gueverra, Nkrumah,
Cabral, Mondlane, and Jackson
that came from the guest speakers lips:
—"UMOJA means unity…
and united are we with the elders,
all long since dead
but alive in our hearts."

I wiped my face
(tears mingled with sweat)
because it was then that I knew
that I didn't belong.
A body unseen
and a voice unheard…
to be remembered
once a year in celebre.
Having walked the road of the elders…
alive…
I could not be with them.

It's Roomy

my room
is mean.
it's got a t.v.
radio
nick nacks
and an electric clock.

my room
is mean.
it's got a glass mirror
a porcelain sink
and a toilet.

my room
is mean mean mean!
for it's got me(!)…
controlled
castrated
cold
and confined.

Solitary
(in segregation in my 21st Black Day...three in a row.)

as I lie here
(hear?)
In this solitary prison cell
I hear
the cries of misery...
the cries of frustrated anger...
and the ever present sound
of the countless cell doors
clanging
echoing.
I feel the others
before me
who left something behind them—
some part of themselves here.
and what of the others
after me
who will hear
(here?)
in this solitary
prison cell?

The Raven's Might

Fate once cast a kindred spirit
sail upon the troubled sea,
through my dreams I remember that sail
has always beckoned unto me.

Severe hurricane winds, that maim and rend,
have been in close pursuit.
Now my embarkation, from these old moorings,
becomes all the more resolute.

The sea squalls build an illusion,
tempting me toward the norm.
But, like all sailing ships,
       I have been charted to resort
           to unfamiliar ports
whenever there threatens a storm.

Safe, sallow, harbor lights allure me,
as waves crash across my bow.
Yet,
       I will steer clear,
      because you see, my dear,
I must test my convictions now.

I have noticed the darkening clouds,
and I wonder:
     "When will the tempest breach?"
Then, while I scan the sky,
I realize that only I
     can bring my objectives into reach.
                   Almighty thunder and rain,
                   descend all around me!
                   The atmosphere is

                distempered.
                The environment is amiss.

                My tall spars creak!
                My ebony timbers leak!

                But, I will continue
                to sail on through
                the threatening abyss.

Look to the east,
when dawn is the NEW morning
and sun Ra will reveal this sight:

                The stormy tempest is past,
                and safely harbored, at last,
                lies the weather-worn ship:
                "THE RAVEN'S MIGHT!"

The Price of Recognition

(Written after three Black publishing establishments turned down my manuscript. I harbored the thought of giving up in trying to publish my works at this time.)

will I
have to die
before I am recognized?
           as a poet
           in my own right
           as a soldier
           that still has long to fight
           as a victim
           of the white man's fears
           as a prisoner
           with a hundred years
           as a sacrifice
           for my people's woes
           as amerik.k.k.a struggles
           in its last death throes…

will I
have to die
before I am recognized?

From Where I Live

From where I live
the world seems cold
as I stare at the endless gray
in the expanse of sky that I must look upon
at the beginning of a meaningless day.

For where I live
young men grow old
as the years agonizingly pass by
with kodak pictures turned and cracked by tears
from tired yet ageless eyes.

Now, where I live
it can be said
that men have paid the cost.
our minds and our bodies are systematically bled…
our sanity is regained and then lost.

Die where I live
in an environment
that reminds one of chattel slavery days.
made to reimburse a hostile white society
for a debt that 400 years had already pre-paid.

Corporate Directives

    REJECTION!
Mock the I givers of pure wisdom!
Banish them through ridicule and disgrace,
but praise and adore the "cast of ignorance"
who perform daily in **black face**.

    MACHINATION!
Stifle all reflex and emotion!
It's easy for three-quarters of a human being.
Then change the code in the color spectrum
and classify gun metal grey as forest green.

    POLLUTION!
Gaze upon nature's many wonders;
although you can no longer see the sky
through the soot of life's death industry
and the polluted film that blinds your eyes.

    PROJECTION!
Ration all of your dreams for a better tomorrow!
Pass them out one by one.
Rebate and recycle all of your sorrow...
o mighty children of the sun!

    DESTRUCTION!
Turning the other cheek is a blessing!
Over and over again it has been said,
so, just keep turning and twisting;
being spun until you're dead.

Teardroppings

Reflection in a teardrop
as another year has now fled by.
To have, to me, is to have not
and still I refuse to cry.

Reflection in a teardrop
as another picture has been pasted
in my book of wilted snapshots
taken during the six years I have now wasted.

Detection in a teardrop
of the beauty of my Queen…
this gift that nature has wrought
from my broken wishes, hopes and dreams.

Detection in a teardrop
of a love that is feverishly kindling.
Can the trials and obstacles be overcome when
fought or will our souls be once again wandering?

Oppression in a teardrop
seen as brother feeding upon brother.
Not knowing when this repression will stop
as this year fades into another.

In Memorial

Remember me?
The boy who tried to reach
but my hand was slapped;
tried to strike back
but my arm was trapped.
I'M ALIVE!
Remember me?
I cried that day
when two white men took me away.
Yes, I'm the boy who tried to say:
"I'M ALIVE!"
Remember me?
Those three long years
that they kept me there,
through the physical abuse and the mental despair.
I'M ALIVE!
Remember me?
In 1966 on the street,
our finest hour…
with our dreams of hope
and our screams of "BLACK POWER!!"
I'M ALIVE!
Remember me?
The manchild alone
who said: "I'll fight back."
then became the victim
of a police attack
when I raised a weighted head
and said: "I'M ALIVE."

Remember me?
Well, now in a cell I am
for trying to portray an unafraid Blackman.

I'm physically capped and contained
but my mind is free (?)
and I have a fairly good memory—
I'm uh…
I'm uh…
I'm uh…
I'm alive?!

INDEX OF TITLES AND FIRST LINES

Titles are in bold with first lines in italics.

A baby's cry	34
A Bi-nonsense-terminal Message	31
A Constant Reminder Merits One Shining Example	34
A Hymn...Sung Black for the Bicentennial.	26
All through my childhood	5
Amerik.k.k.a the free?	31
Ancestral spirits spiral up from smoking hamlets —	**13**
as I lie here	51
As the sun	24
As they sang,	48
Born and bred on a ghetto street—	41
Connect the Dots...Subject: Filling the Bill	42
Corporate Directives	57
Cry if he's gone,	23
David's Song	23
Dear Stranger / The Wayfarer	2
D Implications of One	37
Fate once cast a kindred spirit	52
From childhood, society drills into man's head	20
From Where I Live	56
From where I live	56
got letter tonight	21

Happy Horrorday	**44**
Hear a rumbling to the south,	*11*
I am	*2*
I am Somebody	**5**
I cried from the gutter	*25*
In Memorial	**59**
Inspired wisdom of the sages.	*33*
In the beginning	*16*
It's Roomy	**50**
Kwanza...When I Could Not Be With Them	**48**
Mass(achusetts) Sanitation	**25**
my room	*50*
Oh listen youth	*26*
Once upon a time there was a farmer,	*38*
One is a solitary bird—	*37*
One of the Greatest Stories Never Told	**38**
Phoenix	**9**
Pink or Blue	**21**
Preserves	**4**
Reflection in a teardrop	*58*
REJECTION!	*57*
Remember me?	*59*
Santa Claus is coming to town!	*44*
Satan's Sunrise Serenade	**24**
Solitary	**51**
Sphynx	**33**
Teardroppings	**58**

The Ballad of Eritrea	**13**
The Coloring Book	**41**
The First Book of Mankind Called Oblivion	**16**
The Price of Recognition	*55*
The Raven's Might	*52*
The stains on your hands (all up under your nails)	*4*
The Tinderbox	**20**
Thunder in the Transkei	**11**
We are living in the milk and honey land of democracy,	*42*
We played it well	*9*
will I	*55*

ABOUT THE AUTHOR

Ralph C Hamm III

Ralph, born in 1950, is serving a non-capital first offense life sentence for "intent," stemming from a criminal episode that occurred in 1968 – when he was seventeen years old. During his decades of imprisonment he has aided in spearheading Massachusetts' prison reform movement, has earned degrees in liberal arts, divinity, metaphysics, and paralegal; as well as developed into a published poet, playwright, musician, and artist. In 2007 he was acknowledged as a contributor to the book, *When the Prisoners Ran Walpole* by Jamie Bissonette; and is author of *Manumission: The Liberated Consciousness of a Prison(er) Abolitionist*, as well as *Blackberry Juice* and *The Tinderbox*.

WHY DO I WRITE?

I write because a prison needs a poet—a chronicler—someone who has experienced at firsthand the agony of the disenfranchised, and can interpret through his very soul the expression of suffering by the collective whole.

I write because the only way for the public to learn about what it is like to sub-exist within "the bowels of the beast" (the criminal justice system) is to listen to an inhabitant. Not just any inhabitant, but one who understands and can articulate the conditions of his confinement. No criminal psychologist, sociologist, so-called criminal justice professional, nor salaried correctional official knows what it is truly like to venture through the looking-glass of the criminal justice system as a member of the marginalized under-caste in America—unless they have served time themselves.

I write because the Massachusetts Parole Board has told me, after having served over 40 years on a non-capital life sentence, to die in prison because of my beliefs.

I write because I refuse to quietly go to my grave.

I write because my life was offered as a sacrifice upon the altar of criminal justice: as the means to secure and uphold an easy and speedy conviction—to curry favor and gratitude from a race-conscious and vindictive society—to secure a method in the Commonwealth to undermine the Constitutional guarantees to trial by jury and effective assistance of trial counsel…and to forward the careers of those involved with the so-called professional aspects of the case in the Massachusetts legal system.

I write because criminal justice in Massachusetts is told as a one-sided story: where voices of the poor undercaste are seldom, if ever, heard…where there are no second chances, nor room for redemption.

I write because in Massachusetts the courts have declared that it is "reasonable" for skin color to be the determinant factor in coercing juvenile defendants to waive trial by jury—that trial counsel does not have to investigate the facts of a criminal case if he has access to the prosecutor's case file, in spite of the Massachusetts Canon of Ethics—and, as a result, that physical, material, and exculpatory evidence can be withheld or destroyed prior to trial.

I write because juvenile first time offenders such as myself can receive life sentences for non capital offenses, because he is "black and his victims white" …that an adult codefendant, and ringleader of said criminal episode, can enter into a secret sentencing deal with the Commonwealth, testify against and inculcate a juvenile codefendant, and thereby be released from charges against a female victim and returned to the community to commit even more egregious crimes…that victims can be convinced to lie, without having to face cross-examination from trial counsel, because counsel has determined that the victims have been through enough already.

I write because it is the desire of the criminal justice system to have its victims suffer in obscurity, to be tortured away from prying eyes and a possible scrutiny by the mass media; thereby absolving society from any plausible charge of injustice, as well as from the realization that the social conditions that birth criminal behavior are responsible for crime.

I write because America is a country whose social reality is viewed by most through the prism of rose-tinted glasses, after first being distorted by a series of Fun House mirrors and smokescreens…a society where the Voters' Rights Act of 1965 and 1970 must be continually renewed by a sitting President, in an effort to guarantee that black people (the descendants of slaves) maintain their right to vote…a country where one of the by-products of mass incarceration, in several states, is a lifetime of disenfranchisement of the right to vote and the methodology utilized by politicos to circumvent the Voters' Rights Acts.

I write because in spite of America's bombast proclaiming freedom and liberty for all, the 13th Amendment to the U.S. Constitution holds an authorized exception to the abolition of slavery which is rigidly enforced and exploited.

I write because.

WHAT DO I WRITE ABOUT?

I write about how the Massachusetts criminal justice system is criminal to the degree where it is not a system of justice, it is a system of "just-us." The system is designed to fool enough of the general public enough of the time to justify its disparities against racial minorities and the poor. It is a system of "just-us" that reserves its severest penalties and sentences for its lower income/caste members of society, except when the violations of the law are bartered with informants and/or members of organized crime tendered by a rose in a fisted kid glove.

For example, I write about: in what other system of social control can a black juvenile first time offender receive a life sentence for intending to commit a crime, as well as receive a consecutive life sentence for his involvement in a $20.00 robbery of an emphasized white person, and thereby serve over 44 years in prison: while a white organized crime hit-man can confess to killing 22 people, barter and serve only 12 years in prison, and be released back into society as an avowed serial killer; and the black juvenile's trial/defense attorney (as a white member of yet another aspect of organized crime in this State) can rob a client of $100,000.00 from an estate, barter, and not serve one minute in prison?

I write about the benefits of the criminal "just-us" system serving as an economic advantage for the middle and upper castes, and the social institutions at work to maintain rather than eliminate crime—to reinforce the levels of caste in society. Why must crime be maintained? It is essential to have a visible (black) criminal population as a boundary by which to establish a cultural identity in society, and to sustain a solidarity amongst those who share that cultural identity. Criminal "just-us" is nothing more than a system of perpetual regulations and mirages used to marginalize the disenfranchised poor as scapegoats for society's shortcomings.

www.ingramcontent.com/pod-product-compliance
Lightning Source LLC
Chambersburg PA
CBHW070654050426
42451CB00008B/353